Nelson Comprehension

Pupil Book 4

OXFORD
UNIVERSITY PRESS

OXFORD
UNIVERSITY PRESS

Great Clarendon Street, Oxford, OX2 6DP, United Kingdom

Oxford University Press is a department of the University of Oxford. It furthers the University's objective of excellence in research, scholarship, and education by publishing worldwide. Oxford is a registered trade mark of Oxford University Press in the UK and in certain other countries

British Library Cataloguing in Publication Data
Data available
ISBN: 978-0-19-836819-9

10 9 8 7 6 5 4 3

Paper used in the production of this book is a natural, recyclable product made from wood grown in sustainable forests. The manufacturing process conforms to the environmental regulations of the country of origin.

Printed in China by Golden Cup

Acknowledgements
Cover illustration: Briony May Smith

Illustrations: Maurizio De Angelis, Robin Lawrie, Wes Lowe, Ivan Vazquez , Topics, p.4: Zosia Dzierżawska, pp.6–8: Joe Lillington, pp.32–33: Sarah Edmonds, pp.46–47: Joe Lillington, p.56: Zosia Dzierżawska and p.58: Briony May Smith.

Photographs: p10: Alamy Stock Photo; p12(t): FRANCK FIFE/AFP/Getty Images; p12(b): Bikeworldtravel / Shutterstock; p14: Martin Good / Shutterstock; Stefan Holm / Shutterstock; Rihardzz / Shutterstock; p22: Fotolia; p24: Fotolia; p26: tororo reaction / Fotolia; p27: Fotolia; p34: Jacek Chabraszewski / Fotolia; p42: BBC Photo Library; p48(t): Pictorial Press Ltd / Alamy; p48(b): Patrick Guenette / Alamy.

The author and publisher are grateful to the following for permission to reprint copyright material:

Nina Bawden: extract from *Carrie's War* (Puffin, 2014), copyright © Nina Bawden 1974, reprinted by permission of Curtis Brown, London on behalf of the Estate of Nina Mary Kark; Ann Cameron: extract from *The Most Beautiful Place in the World* (Tamarind, 2014), text copyright © Ann Cameron 1988, reprinted by permission of The Random House Group Ltd and Alfred A Knopf, an imprint of Random House Children's Books, a division of Penguin Random House LLC. All rights reserved; Anita Desai: extract from *The Peacock Garden* (Mammoth, 1991) copyright © Anita Desai 1979, reprinted by permission of the author c/o Rogers Coleridge & White Ltd, 20 Powis Mews, London W11 1JN; Berlie Doherty: 'Quieter than Snow' from *Walking on Air* (Hodder Children's Books 1999), reprinted by permission of David Higham Associates; Rachel Field: 'The Hills' from *Poems of Childhood* (Atheneum, 1996), copyright © Macmillan Publishing Company 1934, copyright renewed 1962 by Arthur S Pederson, reprinted by permission of Atheneum Books for Young Readers, an imprint of Simon & Schuster Children's Publishing Division; Alan Gibbons: extract from *Chicken* (Dent, 1993), copyright © Alan Gibbons 1993, reprinted by permission of Orion Children's Books, an imprint of the Hachette Children's Group, London; Dennis Hamley: extract from *The War and Freddy* (Catnip, 2007), copyright © Dennis Hamley 1991, reprinted by permission of the author; David Harmer: 'One Moment in Summer', copyright © David Harmer 2005, first published in *The Works 4: every kind of poem on every topic* chosen by Pie Corbett & Gaby Morgan (Macmillan Children's Books, 2005), reprinted by permission of the author; C S Lewis: extract from *The Lion the Witch and The Wardrobe* (G Bles, 1950), copyright © C S Lewis Pt. Ltd, 1950, reprinted by permission of The C S Lewis Company; Kenneth Lillington: extract from *The Hallowe'en Cat* (Faber, 1987), copyright © Kenneth Lillington 1987, reprinted by permission of Faber & Faber Ltd; Beverley Naidoo: extract from *Journey to Jo'Burg* (Pearson Longman, 2008), copyright © Beverley Naidoo 1995, reprinted by permission of The Agency (London) Ltd. All rights reserved and enquiries to The Agency (London) Ltd, 24 Pottery Lane, London W11 4LZ; J R R Tolkien: extract from *The Lord of the Rings: The Fellowship of the Ring* (G Allen & Unwin 1954), copyright © The Tolkien Estate Ltd 1937, 1965, reprinted by permission of HarperCollins Publishers Ltd; Robert Westall: extract from *Blitz* (HarperCollins, 2009), copyright © the Estate of Robert Westall, reprinted by permission of Laura Cecil on behalf of the author's Estate.

Any third party use of this material, outside of this publication, is prohibited. Interested parties should apply to the copyright holders indicated in each case.

Although we have made every effort to trace and contact all copyright holders before publication this has not been possible in all cases. If notified, the publisher will rectify any errors or omissions at the earliest opportunity.

Oxford OWL Discover eBooks, inspirational resources, advice and support www.oxfordowl.co.uk

Contents

UNIT 1

Leaving London

Carrie, 12, and her younger brother Nick, 9, are being evacuated from London during the Second World War. They are on a train with their schoolteacher, Miss Fazackerly, going to Wales.

He threw up all over Miss Fazackerly's skirt. He had been feeling sick ever since they left the main junction and climbed into the joggling, jolting little train for the last lap of their journey, but the sudden whistle had finished him.

Such a noise – it seemed to split the sky open. 'Enough to frighten the dead,' Miss Fazackerly said, mopping her skirt and Nick's face with her handkerchief. He lay back limp as a rag and let her do it, the way he always let people do things for him, not lifting a finger. 'Poor lamb,' Miss Fazackerly said, but Carrie looked stern.

'It's all his own fault. He's been stuffing his face ever since we left London.' … He had had all her chocolate, too! 'I knew he'd be sick,' she said smugly.

'Might have warned me then, mightn't you?' Miss Fazackerly said. Not unkindly, she was one of the kindest teachers in the school, but Carrie wanted to cry suddenly. If she had been Nick she would have cried, or at least put on a hurt face. Being Carrie she stared crossly out of the carriage window at the big mountain on the far side of the valley. It was brown and purple on the top and green lower down; streaked with silver trickles of water and dotted with sheep. Sheep and mountains.

'Oh, it'll be such fun,' their mother had said when she kissed them good-bye at the station. 'Living in the country instead of the stuffy old city. You'll love it, you see if you don't!' As if Hitler had arranged this old war for their benefit, just so that Carrie and Nick could be sent away in a train with gas masks slung over their shoulders and their names on cards round their necks. Labelled like parcels – Caroline Wendy Willow and Nicholas Peter Willow – only with no address to be sent to. None of them, not even the teachers, knew where they were going. 'That's part of the adventure,' Carrie's mother had said, and not just to cheer them up: it was her nature to look on the bright side. …

Thinking of her mother, always making the best of things (or pretending to: when the train began to move she had stopped smiling), Carrie nearly did cry. There was a lump like a pill stuck in her throat. She swallowed hard and pulled faces.

The train was slowing. 'Here we are,' Miss Fazackerly said. 'Collect your things, don't leave anything. Take care of Nick, Carrie.'

Carrie's War, **Nina Bawden**

Teach

4

Understanding the text

1 Who are the main characters in the story?

2 What is the setting?

3 Where are they moving to?

4 Why has Nick been sick?

5 Where are they moving from?

Looking at language

6 Choose the correct definition for each of these phrases.

a *finished him*	made him feel better	made him feel worse
b *not lifting a finger*	helping	not helping
c *look on the bright side*	be pessimistic	be optimistic

7 Explain what these words mean as they are used in the story.
Use a dictionary to help you.

a stern   **b** smugly   **c** stuffy   **d** benefit   **e** slung

Exploring the characters

8 We are told Miss Fazackerly is 'kind'. What kind things did she do?

9 What impression do you get of:

a Carrie?   **b** Nick?

10 How do you know that the children's mother is only pretending to make the best of things?

11 Why do you think the children are being sent away from home?

Taking it further

▶ (RB, Unit I, Extension)

12 If you were Nick or Carrie would you think this was an adventure or would you be homesick? Give your reasons.

Teach

UNIT 1

Dad's Double

It is September 1939, during the Second World War. Freddy's father has left to fight in the war and Freddy may never see him again. Freddy watches the enemy planes fly over the town and sees the American soldiers arrive. One day, some other people come …

There were other new arrivals. But they didn't come into the town. Freddy and Stella were walking along the road which passed Farmer Crellin's outlying fields when they saw them. A group of six men, their backs bowed, repairing fences. They wore shabby grey tunics with a yellow circle stitched on the back of each one. A soldier with a rifle stood guarding them. He motioned Stella and Freddy away.

One of the men looked up and stared straight at Freddy.

Freddy's stomach turned over and his legs felt like water.

The man was exactly like his father.

'Da … ' he started to call. But he cut the word off at once.

The man showed no sign of recognition. His face was lined and bitter. Voices murmured. Freddy knew they were speaking in German.

'I'm frightened,' said Stella. 'Let's go home.'

Mum was weeding in the back garden when he returned. Grandads Crake and Bassett were there as well, arguing. Granny Bassett sat in a deck-chair, trying not to listen. Mr Binstead was digging his garden next door. Freddy told them what he'd seen, without mentioning Dad's German double.

'German prisoners of war,' said Mum. 'A few are allowed to work on farms. You must keep away from them.'

Mr Binstead heard.

'A waste of good food,' he shouted over the fence. 'We can do without that lot. If I had my way, they'd all be shot. Serve 'em right after what they've done to us.'

Mum ran indoors, crying.

'Oh, sorry,' said Mr Binstead. 'I forgot.'

'He's a right twerp,' said Grandad Crake.

'He ought to be shot himself,' said Grandad Bassett.

At least they agreed for once.

Freddy dreamed most nights now of his father in a grey tunic working by the side of a road and lines of tanks with white stars on them coming to take him away. And at the back of his dreams was the face of Dad's German double – thin, lined, stubbly-chinned, but with the bitterness in the eyes replaced by yearning at the thought of the many miles between him and his home.

Talk

The War and Freddy, **Dennis Hamley**

Understanding the text

1 What were the men doing when Freddy and Stella first saw them?

2 What was unusual about one of the men?

3 What language were they speaking?

4 What did Mr Binstead think of the prisoners of war?

5 What did Freddy dream about?

Looking at language

6 Explain the meaning of these expressions as they are used in the story.

    a stomach turned over   **b** serve 'em right

7 Explain the meaning of these words as they appear in the story. Use a dictionary to help you.

    a outlying   **b** shabby   **c** recognition
    d twerp   **e** bitterness   **f** yearning

8 What adjectives are used to describe the face of Dad's German double?

9 What impression do these adjectives give you of the man?

Exploring the characters

10 Why do you think the men have a yellow circle stitched on the back of their tunics?

11 Why do you think Stella was frightened?

12 Why do you think Freddy didn't mention 'Dad's German double' at home?

13 Why do you think Freddy's mum ran indoors crying?

14 Do you think Freddy agreed with Mr Binstead's opinion of the prisoners of war or not? Explain your reasons.

Taking it further

▶ (RB, Unit I, Extension)

15 Imagine you could talk to the prisoner who looked like Freddy's Dad. What do you want to know about him? What questions would you ask?

Talk

The Crash

Albert and the narrator are young boys during the Second World War. One day they are playing on an abandoned building site known as Kor. They see a fight in the sky between a German and a British plane. One of the planes crashes …

'Shall we go and look?'

'He might be trapped … He might be …'

It was unsayable. But we went.

It took a long time to search ruined Kor. Expecting at every corner …

But what we found was a surprisingly long way off. A new row of furrows in the field beyond Kor, as if a farmer with six ploughs joined together had …

And a gap in the hedge that something had vanished through. Something definitely British, because a lump of the tail had fallen off, and lay with red, white and blue on it.

We tiptoed through the gap.

It looked as big as a house.

'Spitfire.'

'Hurricane, you idiot. Can't you tell a Spitfire from a Hurricane yet?'

'It's not badly damaged. Just a bit bent.'

I shook my head. 'It'll never fly again. It looks … broke.'

The tail was up in the air; the engine dug right into the ground, and the propeller bent into horseshoe shapes.

'Where's the pilot?'

'He might have baled out,' suggested Albert, hopefully.

'What? At that height? His parachute would never have opened. Reckon he's trapped inside. We'd better have a look.'

'Keep well back,' said Albert. 'There's a terrible smell of petrol. I saw petrol take fire once …'

There was no point in mocking him. I was so scared my own legs wouldn't stop shaking. But it was me that went a yard in front.

The cockpit canopy was closed. Inside, from a distance, there was no sign of any pilot.

'Baled out. Told ya,' said Albert.

'With the canopy closed?'

'The crash could've closed it, stupid.'

'I'm going to have a look.'

I don't think I would have done if I'd thought there was anybody inside. I edged up on the wing, frightened that my steel toe and heel caps would strike a spark from something. The smell of petrol was asphyxiating.

He was inside.

Write

Bent up double, with only the back of his helmet showing. And there was a great tear in the side of the helmet, with leather and stuffing … and blood showing through.

Blitz, **Robert Westall**

1 What were the boys going to look for?

2 How did the boys know that what had 'vanished through the hedge' was 'definitely British'?

3 What were a Hurricane and a Spitfire?

4 Why did Albert say, 'Keep well back'?

5 What did the narrator see in the cockpit?

Looking at language

6 How does the narrator describe the propellers and what does this tell you about them?

7 What does Albert mean when he says, 'I saw petrol take fire once ...'?

8 Explain the meaning of these words as they are used in the story. Use a dictionary to help you.

> **a** unsayable   **b** vanished   **c** baled out
> **d** mocking him   **e** edged up   **f** asphyxiating

Exploring the characters

9 Why do you think the author leaves these sentences unfinished?
   a 'He might be ...'   **b** 'Expecting at every corner ...'

10 Why is the narrator sure that, 'His parachute would never have opened'?

11 The narrator says, 'I was so scared ...' What two things do you think he was scared of?

12 Both boys were frightened but which of them do you think was braver? Why?

13 How would you have felt if you were one of the boys? What would you have done?

Taking it further

 RB, Unit I, Extension

14 Imagine you are the narrator. What would you do and how would you feel if:
   a you found the pilot dead?
   b you found the pilot alive?

Write

Marathon Marvel Hangs up Her Running Shoes

In April 2003, Paula Radcliffe set the world record of 2 hours, 15 minutes and 25 seconds for the London Marathon. Twelve years later, she ran her last London Marathon. At 41 years of age, it was time to hang up her running shoes as far as competitive racing was concerned. She completed the 26.2-mile race in 2 hours, 36 minutes and 55 seconds and received the race's Lifetime Achievement Award.

Born in 1973, in Cheshire, England, Paula suffered from asthma and anaemia as a child. Despite this, she took up running at the age of seven and joined the Frodsham Athletic Club. When she was 12, her family moved to Bedfordshire and she joined the Bedford Athletic Club. At the World Cross Country Championships in 1992, she came first.

Over her illustrious career Paula has won the London Marathon three times, in 2002, 2003 and 2005; the New York Marathon in 2004, 2007 and 2008; and the Chicago Marathon in 2002. She has also been victorious over 5,000 and 10,000 metre distances and Cross Country races.

Due to her many achievements, the British public took Paula to their hearts and voted her the BBC Sports Personality of the Year in 2003. Radcliffe has attracted a legion of fans. Kim Thomas, who has seen every London Marathon and travelled all over the world to watch Paula run said, 'She is truly amazing. It takes such strength and determination to compete as she does. I think long-distance running must be the hardest sport there is.'

Early on in her career, Paula outlined her attitude to her sport. 'I'm not looking to make a living out of it. Obviously it's nice that there's a bit of money coming in but that's not my goal. I just want to do my best and still enjoy it. I want to keep on enjoying it, keep on improving, get as much out of it as I can and put as much back as I can.'

The *Daily Express* recognised that 'she deserves her place as one of the world's greats of athletics' and the *Daily Mail* claimed she is 'Britain's greatest ever woman athlete'. Few would say they were wrong.

Tom Phillips
Sports Correspondent

Teach

Understanding the text

1 What is the article about?

2 How long did it take for Paula to run the London Marathon:
   a in 2003?
   b twelve years later?

3 Where was Paula born?

4 What did she suffer from as a child?

5 How many times did she win:
   a the London Marathon?   b the New York Marathon?
   c the Chicago Marathon?

Looking at language

6 The article tells us that the British people 'took Paula to their hearts'.
   Explain in your own words how people felt about her.

7 Explain the meaning of these words as they are used in the article.
   Use a dictionary to help you.

   a anaemia   b illustrious   c victorious
   d legion   e determination   f outlined

Exploring the article

8 Find evidence in the article that suggests Paula will not stop running entirely.

9 How do you know that Kim Thomas is a keen fan of the sport?

10 Do you think it is a good headline? Why? Why not?

11 There are six paragraphs in the article. Briefly summarise what each one
    is about.

12 Give an example from the article of:
    a a fact.   b an opinion.

13 Explain in your own words Paula's attitude to her sport.

Taking it further

▶ (RB, Unit 2, Extension)

14 If you could interview Paula Radcliffe, what questions would you ask her?

Teach

On Your Bike

Pedestrians do not like cyclists on the pavement. Drivers do not like cyclists on the road. But love them or hate them, cyclists are not only here to stay, but are increasing in number at a rapid rate.

Large cities, small cities, towns and villages – all are seeing more and more people choose cycling over other forms of transport. So what is causing people to leave their cars at home, shun public transport and get on their bikes? Four of the reasons are cost, time, health and the environment.

Petrol prices go up and down but, even at its lowest, petrol is still expensive. Add to that the cost of parking when you have reached your destination and the cost of a journey soon mounts up.

Public transport is an alternative to the car but it can often increase the journey time. Buses are often late and trains can be delayed or cancelled.

Cycling is a great form of exercise and helps people keep fit. Some people say it helps the planet, as they see cycling as 'greener' than transport that uses petrol and diesel.

Over the past few years, however, there has been another reason. The success of the British Cycling Team in Olympics and World Championships over recent years has made many people become enthusiastic about cycling.

Government and local authorities are also doing their bit. More cycle lanes are being created on busy roads, and cycle training in schools is being reintroduced.

So, with all these benefits, and the inspiration of the British Cycling Team, there is no reason not to GET ON YOUR BIKE!

Sally Davis
Transport Correspondent

Understanding the text

1 Who wrote the article?
2 What is it about?
3 How many reasons does the article give for more people cycling?
4 List the reasons.
5 What are being created on busy roads?

Looking at language

6 Explain these phrases in your own words.

   a here to stay   **b** soon mounts up   **c** doing their bit

7 Explain these words as they are used in the article. Use a dictionary to help you.

   a pedestrians   **b** rapid   **c** shun   **d** destination
   e greener   **f** delayed   **g** enthusiastic   **h** inspiration

8 What can the expression 'on your bike' sometimes mean?
   What does it mean here?

Exploring the article

9 The article says that both pedestrians and drivers 'do not like cyclists'.
   What do you think are the reasons for this?
10 The article gives reasons for why people are using bicycles more and more.
   Which do you think is the best reason? Why?
11 Give an example from the article of:

   a a fact.   **b** an opinion.
12 What are the disadvantages of public transport?
13 How do you know that there used to be cycle training in schools?
14 Do you think this is a good idea? Why? Why not?

Taking it further   ▶ (RB, Unit 2, Extension)

15 Your school is going to begin cycle-training lessons.
   Design a flyer on A4 paper for parents including the following information.
   a when and where the training will be
   b what equipment is needed
   c why it is important that children learn to ride a bicycle properly
   d why cycling is good for the environment

   You want people to read it and not just throw it away. Think of a good   **Talk**
   headline and make the flyer eye-catching.

Three Times the Pain!

David Franks, our Sports Correspondent, has been investigating the sport known as the 'triathlon'. Introduced into the Olympic Games in 2000, it is one of the most gruelling tests of fitness and stamina.

Swimmers, cyclists and runners are among the fittest athletes in the world. Each sport demands vigorous training, a controlled diet and plenty of stamina and determination.

So, just imagine, in one race, you have to swim, cycle and run without stopping! Well, that's what triathletes do!

The race begins with a 1.5 kilometre swim. You are not in a warm swimming pool sheltered from wind, rain or soaring temperatures. This is in open water – a freezing lake or across a harbour.

After swimming (no time to get dry!), you have to be ready to cycle 40 kilometres. This is not in a flat, indoor velodrome, but on the open road with all its climbs, twists and turns, and weather!

After getting off your bicycle – if you can manage that – there is still the 10 kilometre run to complete. This is not

on a purpose-built running track but, again, on the open road.

So, why do people put themselves through this? One young triathlete, Luke Read, told me, 'For me, it's all about the challenge. If you get into this sport, you are probably good at one of the disciplines, but not so good at the others. You have to train hard at all three. It's no good being the faster swimmer if you can't cycle very fast. It's no good being great at the 10 kilometre run, if you climb out of the water way behind the others. It's keeping the three things going and always trying to get better.'

Do you think a triathlon is for you? I'll stick to writing about it!

Understanding the text

1 Who wrote the article?

2 What is it about?

3 How many different sports are involved? List them in order.

4 When did the triathlon become an Olympic sport?

Looking at language

5 Explain these words as they are used in the article. Use a dictionary to help you.

a gruelling   b stamina   c vigorous
d determination e velodrome   f disciplines

6 Explain these phrases in your own words.

a soaring temperatures   b purpose-built   c get into

Exploring the article

7 Why do you think the article is called *Three Times the Pain!*?

8 What is the total distance the athletes cover in a triathlon?

9 Which do you think is the hardest part of the race? Explain your reasons.

10 Why do you think David Franks included what Luke Read told him?

11 The article is in seven paragraphs.
Briefly summarise what each paragraph is about.

12 What sort of triathlete do you think has the best chance of winning the race?

Taking it further

▶ (RB, Unit 2, Extension)

13 Think about the three newspaper articles you have read.
Choose the one you like best.
Write a paragraph to say why you thought it was interesting.

Write

Quieter Than Snow

I went to school a day too soon
And couldn't understand
Why silence hung in the yard like sheets
Nothing to flap or spin, no creaks
Or shocks of voices, only air.

And the car park empty of teachers' cars
Only the first September leaves
Dropping like paper. No racks of bikes
No kicking legs, no fights,
No voices, laughter, anything.

Yet the door was open. My feet
Sucked down the corridor. My reflection
Walked with me past the hall.
My classroom smelt of nothing. And the silence
Rolled like thunder in my ears.

At every desk a child stared at me
Teachers walked through walls and back again
Cupboard doors swung open, and out crept
More silent children, and still more.

They tiptoed round me
Touched me with ice-cold hands
And opened up their mouths with laughter
That was

Quieter than snow.

Berlie Doherty

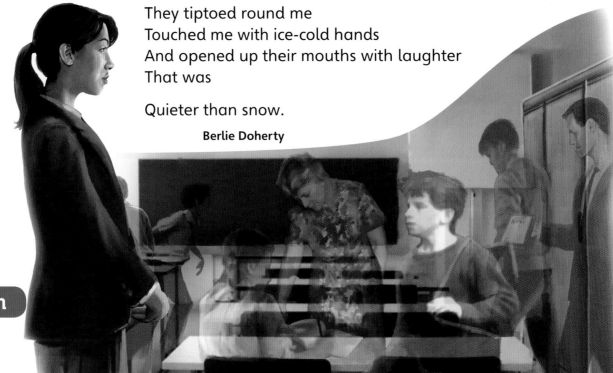

Understanding the text

1 What is the title of the poem?

2 When did the poet go to school?

3 What was the poet expecting to see and hear at school?

4 What did the poet see outside?

5 What did the poet see in the classroom?

Looking at language

6 What does the poet say the silence was like:

    a in the yard?   **b** in the classroom?

7 Why do you think these descriptions are different?

8 Find the similes which describe the following.

    a the leaves   **b** the laughter

9 Explain why you think these descriptions are good or not.

10 The poet says, 'My feet / Sucked down the corridor'. What impression does the word 'sucked' give you?

Exploring the poem

11 Who do you think the children and the teachers are?

12 How do you think the poet felt when:
    a she arrived at school?
    b she arrived in the classroom?

13 How does the poem make you feel?

Taking it further

▶ RB, Unit 3, Extension

14 If you could talk to the children, what would you say? What would you want to know?

Teach

The Hills

Sometimes I think the hills
That loom across the harbour
Lie there like sleeping dragons,
Crouched one above another,
With trees for tufts of fur
Growing all up and down
The ridges and humps of
their backs,
And orange cliffs for claws
Dipped in the sea below.

Sometimes a wisp of smoke
Rises out of the hollows,
As if in their dragon sleep
They dreamed of strange
old battles.
What if the hills should stir
Some day and stretch themselves,
Shake off the clinging trees
And all the clustered houses?

Rachel Field

Talk

Understanding the text

1 What does the poet think the hills could be?

2 What do the trees look like?

3 What do the orange cliffs look like?

4 What are they dreaming of?

5 What does the poet wonder about in the last four lines of the poem?

Looking at language

6 Explain the meaning of these words as they are used in the poem.
Use a dictionary to help you.

> **a** loom   **b** crouched   **c** wisp
>
> **d** hollows   **e** stir   **f** clustered

Exploring similes and metaphors

7 The hills the poet is describing are 'across the harbour'. Do you think they are very near or at a distance? Explain your reasons.

8 If the poet walked towards the hills, would they look:
   a more like dragons?   **b** less like dragons?

Explain your answer.

9 What do you think the 'wisp of smoke' could be in the poet's imagination?

10 What do you think it actually is?

11 Why do you think the dragons would be 'dreaming of old battles'?

12 How do you think the poet would feel if, one day, 'the hills should stir'?

Taking it further

 (RB, Unit 3, Extension)

13 Look out of your classroom window and half-close your eyes.

You may be looking at buildings or fields, trees or roads.
In your imagination, what animal can you see?
Describe the parts of your animal. What can you compare each part
of your animal to?

Talk

One Moment in Summer

The house is dropping swallows
one by one from under the gutter

they swoop and fall
on our heads as we queue
for ice cream.

It is so hot
that the long line of cars clogging the road
hums like a line of electric fires.

They shine and shimmer, stink of oil and warm seats
the children gaze out from their misted windows.

Trapped under glass
hair plastered down with sweat
gasping for air like frogs under ice.

The cars crawl round the curve
of the road, stuck in between the shop
and the café.

My ice cream is butterscotch and almond
Lizzie's is chocolate, Harriet's vanilla.

They are so delicious and cold
we lick them slowly, letting the long, cool flavours
slide down our tongues.

Inside the cars, the red-faced people
begin to boil.

The swallows flit and dart
rapid specks of blue, black and white
the summer flies at us
like an arrow.

David Harmer

Understanding the text

1 In the poem, what are:
   a the poet and her friends doing?
   b the cars doing?
   c the people in the cars doing?

2 How do the cars smell?

3 What three flavours of ice cream do the poet and her friends buy?

4 How do they eat the ice cream?

5 What colours are the swallows?

Looking at language

6 Explain in your own words 'the house is dropping swallows'.

7 Find two examples of alliteration in the poem.

8 Explain the meaning of these words as they are used in the poem.
   Use a dictionary to help you.

a swoop	**b** clogging	**c** plastered
d gasping	**e** flit	**f** dart

Exploring words that create images

9 What similes does the poet use to describe:
   a the long line of cars?   **b** the people in the cars?

10 Make a list of all the 'cold' words the poet uses.

11 Make a list of all the 'hot' words the poet uses.

12 Why do you think the poet uses so many 'hot' words?

13 Look at the title of the poem. Do you think it is a good title or not?
   Give your reasons.

Taking it further   ▶ RB, Unit 3, Extension

14 Write a short description called 'One Moment in Winter'.
   It is very cold. You and your friends are queuing for hot drinks.
   The traffic is moving very slowly because there is lots of snow.
   Use as many 'cold' words as you can in your description.

Write

Let's Find Out About Argentina

Location

Argentina is the second largest country in South America. It is long and thin with a 4,989 kilometre coastline which joins the Atlantic Ocean. It has borders with Bolivia, Brazil, Chile, Paraguay and Uruguay.

Terrain

Much of the northern part of the country is 'pampas'. This is a Spanish word meaning a flat, featureless area. Along the western border of the country are the Andes. The highest point in this mountain range is Cerro Aconcagua which rises to 6,960 metres. There can be earthquakes in this part of the Andes.

Climate

Most of the country has a temperate climate. However, the south east is arid and the south west very cold, as this is the nearest point to the Antarctic. Violent wind storms can hit the northern part of the country.

The people

The population of Argentina is estimated to be 43 million. The official language is Spanish, but Italian, English, German and French are also widely spoken. As Argentina exports wheat, maize and enormous quantities of meat, many people work on the land.

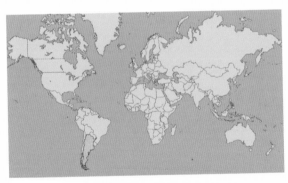

Buenos Aires is the capital city of Argentina. More than a third of the country's population live and work here.

BOLIVIA
BRAZIL
Pacific Ocean
PARAGUAY
Andes
Cerro Aconcagua
URUGUAY
CHILE
Buenos Aires
ARGENTINA
Atlantic Ocean
ANTARTIC

1 What is the information text about?

2 Where is Argentina?

3 What is the name of the mountain range in Argentina?

4 Which part of the country is very cold? Why?

5 What is the capital city?

Looking at language

6 Explain the meaning of these words as they are used in the text. Use a dictionary to help you.

a coastline   **b** featureless   **c** temperate
d arid   **e** population   **f** exports

7 'The official language is Spanish'. What do you understand by the 'official language' of a country?

8 Why do you think the population is only 'estimated'?

Exploring the information

9 How has the writer organised the information?

10 What is the main title of the information text?

11 Give an example of a subheading.

12 As well as using words, what else has the writer included to give the reader information? How are these useful?

13 Make a list of questions showing what else you would like to know about Argentina.

14 Who do you think would be interested in reading this information text?

Taking it further

▶ (RB, Unit 4, Extension)

Teach

15 Would you like to visit Argentina? Why? Why not?

Let's Find Out About China

Location

China's official name is The People's Republic of China. It is in eastern Asia with coastlines along the East China Sea, the Yellow Sea, the Korea Bay and the South China Sea. It shares borders with many other countries including India and Russia.

Terrain

China is a very mountainous country with high plateaus. There are deserts in the west of the country and hills in the east. Mount Everest, the highest mountain in the world, is on China's western border with Nepal.

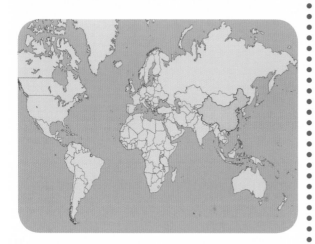

Climate

China is a huge country and has many different climates. It is tropical in the south and very cold in the north. It has frequent typhoons along its southern and eastern coasts. It experiences droughts, floods and tsunamis.

The people

The population of China is over 1.3 billion people. Its main language is standard Chinese or Mandarin but many other dialects, such as Cantonese, are spoken. Its capital city is Beijing, where the 2008 Olympic Games were held.

Talk

Understanding the text

1 What is China's official name?

2 Name one of the seas along its coastline.

3 Where are China's deserts?

4 What is the climate like in the north of the country?

5 What is China's main language?

Looking at language

6 Find the adjectives in the text that are made from these nouns.

a the east   b the south   c the west

7 Explain the meaning of these words as they are used in the information text. Use a dictionary to help you.

a official   b mountainous   c plateaus
d tropical   e frequent   f typhoons

Exploring the information

8 What is the title of the information text?

9 Why do you think the writer has used subheadings? Are they useful or not? Why?

10 Why do you think the writer has included a map?

11 What information have you found out about Mount Everest?

12 Why do you think China has 'many different climates'?

13 What other information could the writer have included which you would find interesting?

14 Would you like to visit China or not? Explain your reasons.

Taking it further

 RB, Unit 4, Extension

15 Choose a country that you are interested in or have visited. Make a list of questions showing what information you would like to know about this country.

Talk

Let's Find Out About Australia

Location

Australia is in the southern hemisphere. Its coastline is 34,218 kilometres in length and it does not border any other country.

Terrain

Australia is mostly low plateaus, and deserts cover most of the land away from the coast. It has a fertile plain in the south-east. Just off the coastline to the east can be found the Great Barrier Reef. This is the largest coral reef in the world.

Climate

Most of Australia has a very arid climate. Towards the south it is more temperate, with a climate similar to places like Spain and Italy. The north has a tropical climate. Sometimes there are serious cyclones along the coast, bringing floods and causing damage. The country often experiences drought.

The people

The population of Australia is over 22 million. Europeans began to explore Australia in the 17th century. Many of the people today are descended from European settlers and about 76 per cent of the population speaks English. Other languages include Chinese, Italian and Greek.

The Great Barrier Reef

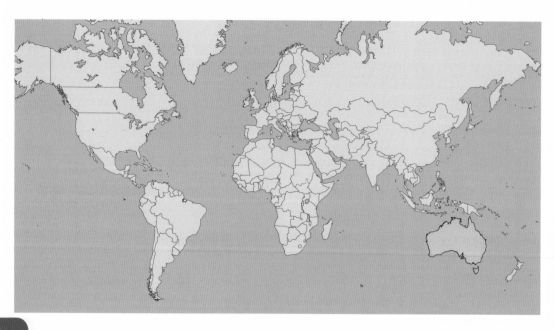

Understanding the text

1 Where is Australia?

2 Where is the Great Barrier Reef?

3 What sort of climate does most of Australia have?

4 How many people live there?

5 What language do most people speak?

Looking at language

6 Explain in your own words 'Many of the people today are descended from European settlers'.

7 The Great Barrier Reef is 'just off the coastline'. Does this mean it is near the coastline or a long way off?

8 Explain the meaning of these words as they are used in the text. Use a dictionary to help you.

a hemisphere		**b** fertile		**c** coral reef	
d cyclones		**e** drought		**f** explore	

Exploring the information

9 In what ways has the writer presented the information?

10 How do you know that Australia is an island?

11 Where do you think most of the food is grown?

12 Where do you think most of the people in Australia live? Why?

13 What other information could the writer have included which you would find interesting?

14 Would you like to visit Australia or not? Give your reasons.

Taking it further   ▶ (RB, Unit 4, Extension)

15 These are three of the main cities in Australia.
   a Canberra   **b** Sydney   **c** Melbourne
   Choose one of these cities.
   What information would you like to know about this city?
   Make a list of questions. Can you find the answers?

Write

Webbo

Davy has arrived at Webbo's school in Liverpool, and Webbo has decided he's an easy target for bullying.

Why me? Why had he taken such an instant dislike to me?

The term's first rounders match had got me off to a bad start, of course. I remember Webbo yelling 'Get it!' Well, how was I to know Lianne Whalley would sky the ball straight at me just when I was busy watching the seagulls pecking the leftover crisps off the Infants' yard? I didn't ask to be in the vital place at the last match-deciding moment. Five rounders each and only my hands between victory and defeat.

'Catch the thing!' bawled Webbo as he raced toward me. I didn't, of course. I tried. I stuck out my hands and did my best to cup them under the ball. I suppose my big chance to be a hero was just too much for me. I closed my eyes and hoped for the best, but the ball popped out of my hands as easily as it had dropped in. Lianne completed the rounder with her arms raised in triumph, while Pete Moran laughed himself sick at my attempt at a catch. Webbo wasn't laughing. He only played to win, and I'd just scuppered his hopes. Webbo didn't like being on the losing side – *ever.*

'You,' hissed Webbo, prodding a finger into my chest. 'You are dead.'

No, he definitely did not like being on the losing side. I looked around. Nobody was listening, nobody except Craig, and he just grimaced sympathetically.

'Try to keep out of Webbo's way,' he advised on the way back into school.

That was easier said than done. I'd realized on my first day since the move from Yorkshire a few months back that Webbo and I weren't going to get on.

'Hey, Woollyback,' he had shouted in the playground.

I must have looked blank.

'Yes, you,' he said. 'Don't you know what a Woollyback is?'

I shook my head. That was a mistake.

'Well, soft lad,' explained Webbo. 'It's like this. There are two kinds of people in the world, Scousers and Woollybacks. If you don't come from Liverpool, then you're a Woollyback. You're not from Liverpool, are you?'

No, I wasn't. I'd finally discovered that I had something in common with Michael Jackson, Arnold Schwarzenegger, the Pope and Mother Teresa of Calcutta – we're all Woollybacks!

'So now you understand, don't you, Woollyback?'

I nodded and turned to walk away. Carl O'Rourke barred my way.

'Who said you could go?' demanded Webbo.

'Nobody,' I admitted. Silly me, I didn't know I needed permission!

'Then you wait till you're told you can go,' said Webbo. 'Understand?'

'Yes,' I murmured nervously. 'I understand.'

Chicken, **Alan Gibbons**

Understanding the text

1 Who are the main characters?

2 Who is narrating the story?

3 Give two reasons why Webbo does not like the narrator.

4 Why didn't the narrator catch the ball?

5 Why was the catch so important?

Looking at language

6 Explain the meaning of these words as they are used in the story. Use a dictionary to help you.

a vital	**b** triumph	**c** scuppered
d grimaced	**e** demanded	**f** permission

7 Explain these expressions in your own words.

a easier said than done   **b** something in common

Exploring the characters

8 How can you tell that Craig is not a member of Webbo's gang but Carl is?

9 The writer uses synonyms for 'said' to show the way the characters speak. Find two examples of how Webbo speaks.

10 What do these synonyms tell about Webbo's character?

11 Do you think Webbo has good reasons for disliking Davy? Why? Why not?

12 How do you think Davy feels about Webbo?

13 What advice does Craig give to the narrator? Say why you do or do not agree with that advice.

Taking it further

▶ RB, Unit 5, Extension

14 Webbo is a bully. How would you advise the narrator to deal with the situation?

Teach

UNIT 5

Trouble With Miss Gratwick

Miss Gratwick has taken a disliking to Mike Pilkington, and, one day, when she tells him off unfairly in front of the class, Mike becomes resentful and talks to his friend Chas about getting back at her.

'Pilkington,' said Miss Gratwick, 'is one of those mean and sneaky boys who call out behind their teacher's back.'

She had a very scathing voice, Miss Gratwick. Mike looked sulky. He didn't mind being ticked off if he deserved it, but this was unfair. He'd actually been trying to *help* Miss Gratwick. He'd been on her *side*. Chas had been prodding him in the back and trying to talk to him, and he had turned round to tell him to *shut up*, and this was the thanks he got.

Miss Gratwick turned as if to go on writing on the blackboard, but swung round again on the chance of catching him grinning at his friends. She was suspicious by nature.

But Mike hadn't moved. The class giggled, and Miss Gratwick felt foolish.

She snapped, 'And you can take that nasty look off your face!'

Gleefully, Chas poked him in the back.

'Sneaky boys, sneaky boys,' he whispered. 'Pilkington is one of those mean and sneaky boys …'

Mike edged away and ignored him.

'Neek-y boys, neek-y boys,' said Chas delightedly under his breath. 'Pil-king-ton is wunna-those-mean 'n' neek-y boys …'

Mike turned suddenly and swiped at Chas's face.

'Oh, shut up!'

'Pilkington,' said Miss Gratwick, 'I've had just about enough of you. Come out!'

She gave Mike a painful knock on the head with the knuckle of her bony forefinger, and made him stand behind the blackboard for the rest of the lesson.

'She's got it in for you,' said Chas, as they left school.

'I've got it in for her and all.'

'What you reckon you're going to do, then?'

'You'll see.'

'What?'

'Not going to tell you.'

'I'll believe it when it happens.'

Mike's heart was full of bitterness. He would have liked to murder Miss Gratwick. But he choked back his feelings and changed the subject.

The Hallowe'en Cat, **Kenneth Lillington**

Talk

Understanding the text

1 What does Miss Gratwick accuse Mike of doing?

2 Why does Mike think it is unfair?

3 Who should Miss Gratwick have been cross with?

4 What does Mike do that really gets him into trouble?

5 How does Miss Gratwick punish Mike?

Looking at language

6 Explain these phrases in your own words.

    a suspicious by nature   **b** got it in for you

7 Explain the meaning of these words as they are used in the story. Use a dictionary to help you.

    a scathing   **b** ticked off   **c** ignored   **d** bitterness

Exploring the characters

8 What sort of person do you think Miss Gratwick is?

9 How do you think she treats Mike?

10 What sort of person do you think Chas is?

11 How do you know that Mike and Chas are friends?

12 Do you think this is odd?

13 Why do you think Mike will not tell Chas what he is going to do?

14 What do you think he is going to do?

Taking it further

▶ (RB, Unit 5, Extension)

15 What do you think would be a sensible way of getting Miss Gratwick to stop picking on you? Why may this be a difficult thing to do?

Talk

The Balaclava Boys

*The narrator of this story wants a balaclava so he can be part of the
'Balaclava Boys'. There is only one problem – his mum won't let him have one!*

I knew exactly the kind of balaclava I wanted. One just like Tony's, a sort
of yellowy-brown. His dad had given it to him because of his earache. Mind
you, he didn't like wearing it at first. At school he'd given it to Barry to wear
and got it back before home-time. But all the other lads started asking if
they could have a wear of it, so Tony took it back and said that from then
on nobody but him could wear it, not even Barry. Barry told him he wasn't
bothered because he was going to get a balaclava of his own, and so did
some of the other lads. And that's how it started – the Balaclava Boys.

It wasn't a gang really. I mean they didn't have meetings or anything like
that. They just went around together wearing their balaclavas, and if you
didn't have one you couldn't go around with them. Tony and Barry
were my best friends, but because I didn't have a balaclava,
they wouldn't let me go round with them. I tried.

'Aw, go on, Barry, let us walk round
with you.'

'No, you can't. You're not a Balaclava Boy.'

'Aw, go on.'

'No.'

'Please.'

I don't know why I wanted to walk round
with them anyway. All they did was wander
up and down the playground dressed in their
rotten balaclavas. It was daft.

'Go on, Barry, be a sport.'

'I've told you. You're not a Balaclava Boy. You've got to have a balaclava. If
you get one, you can join.'

'But I can't, Barry. My mum won't let me have one.'

'Hard luck.'

'You're rotten.'

Then he went off with the others. I wasn't half fed up. All my friends
were in the Balaclava Boys. All the lads in my class except me. Wasn't fair. The
bell went for the next lesson – ooh heck, handicraft with the Miseryguts Garnett
– then it was home-time. All the Balaclava Boys were going in and I
followed them.

'Hey, Tony, do you want to go down to the woods after school?'

'No, I'm going round with the Balaclava Boys.'

'Oh.'

Blooming Balaclava Boys. Why wouldn't *my mum* buy *me a
balaclava*? Didn't she realize that I was losing all my friends, and just
because she wouldn't buy me one?

Write

The Balaclava Story, **George Layton**

32

Understanding the text

1 Why did Tony's dad give him a balaclava?

2 Who are the narrator's best friends?

3 What did the Balaclava Boys do together?

4 Why didn't the narrator have a balaclava?

5 What didn't his mum realize?

Looking at language

6 Explain these phrases in your own words.

a wasn't bothered   b go round with   c be a sport

7 Explain these words as they are used in the story. Use a dictionary to help you.

a rotten   b daft   c fed up   d handicraft

Exploring the characters

8 Tony didn't like his balaclava at first. What made him change his mind?

9 Why does the narrator say that the Balaclava Boys 'wasn't a gang really'?

10 Do you think the way Tony and Barry treated the narrator was fair? Why? Why not?

11 The narrator says that what the Balaclava Boys did was 'daft'. How do you know he didn't really mean this?

12 Why do you think it was so important to the narrator that he had a balaclava?

13 The boys in the balaclavas went around together. Do you think this is a sensible way to choose your friends? Why? Why not?

Taking it further

▶ (RB, Unit 5, Extension)

14 Imagine you are the narrator. You have to explain to your mum why you want a balaclava and persuade her to buy you one. Write how you would do this.

Write

UNIT 6

How Does Your Heart Work?

What is the heart?

The heart is a crucial organ of the body. It pumps blood through the small tubes that we call veins and arteries. Without blood we could not survive.

How does it work?

1   One artery takes blood from the heart to the lungs.
2   When the blood reaches the lungs it picks up oxygen. It leaves carbon dioxide behind in the lungs.
3   The blood with the oxygen goes back to the heart.
4   The other artery takes the blood with the oxygen all around the body.
5   After the oxygen has been delivered, veins bring the blood back to the heart.
6   The process starts all over again.
7   One artery takes blood from the heart to the lungs …

And so the heart pumps the blood around our body, supplying the oxygen that is essential to keep us fit and healthy.

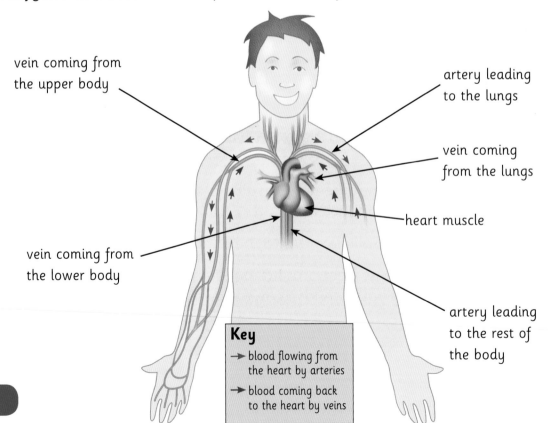

vein coming from the upper body

artery leading to the lungs

vein coming from the lungs

heart muscle

vein coming from the lower body

artery leading to the rest of the body

Key
→ blood flowing from the heart by arteries
→ blood coming back to the heart by veins

Teach

Understanding the text

1 What does the heart do to the blood?

2 What does the blood travel through?

3 Where do arteries take the blood?

4 Where do the veins take the blood?

5 What does the blood take from the lungs? What does it leave behind?

Looking at language

6 Explain the meaning of these words as they are used in the text.
Use a dictionary to help you.

    a crucial   **b** organ   **c** survive
    d delivered   **e** process   **f** essential

Exploring the information

7 What is the purpose of this piece of writing?

8 Who do you think would want to read this?

9 How is the information presented?

10 Why do you think the writer has used:
    a subheadings?   **b** numbers?

11 Is the diagram useful? Why? Why not?

12 Why do you think the writer has included the photograph of a boy jumping?

13 Did you find this explanation easy to understand or not? Explain your reasons.

Taking it further

▶ (RB, Unit 6, Extension)

14 Look carefully at the explanation.
What else would you like to know about the heart and how it works?
Make a list of questions. Can you find the answers?

Teach

How Do We Move?

This is what it looks like inside your arm.

There are:

- bones
- muscles
- joints
- tendons
- ligaments

ligaments hold joints together

muscle and bone are joined by tendons

muscles pull on bones at the joints

joint between two bones

Here is how all these parts work together so you can move your arm. Muscles work in pairs. Muscles A and B work together. Muscles C and D work together.

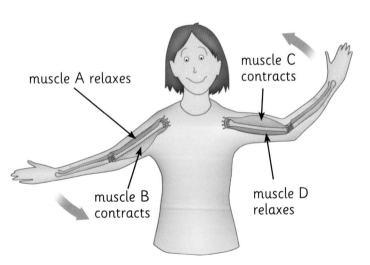

muscle C contracts

muscle A relaxes

muscle B contracts

muscle D relaxes

1 When we want to move our arm downwards, one muscle contracts and the other muscle relaxes. Look at muscles A and B.

2 When we want to move our arm upwards, one muscle contracts and the other muscle relaxes. Look at muscles C and D.

Talk

Understanding the text

1 Name the parts inside your arm.

2 What is it called where two bones meet?

3 What do ligaments do?

4 Do muscles work alone? How do they work?

5 When the parts inside your arm work together, what can you do?

Looking at language

6 Define these words as they are used in the explanation.
Use a dictionary to help you.

a tendons   **b** ligaments   **c** contracts   **d** relaxes

Exploring the information

7 What is the purpose of this piece of writing?

8 Who do you think would want to read this?

9 How is the information presented?

10 Would the explanation be as easy to understand without the diagrams? Why? Why not?

Taking it further

▶ (RB, Unit 6, Extension)

11 Your leg works in the same way as your arm.

- Move the bottom half of your leg upwards. Which muscle is contracting and which muscle is relaxing?

- Move the bottom part of your leg downwards. Which muscle is contracting and which muscle is relaxing?

12 Draw a diagram to explain what you have found out.

Talk

UNIT 6

How Do Our Lungs Work?

This is what it looks like inside your chest.

There are:

- lungs

- windpipe

- heart

- ribs

- muscles

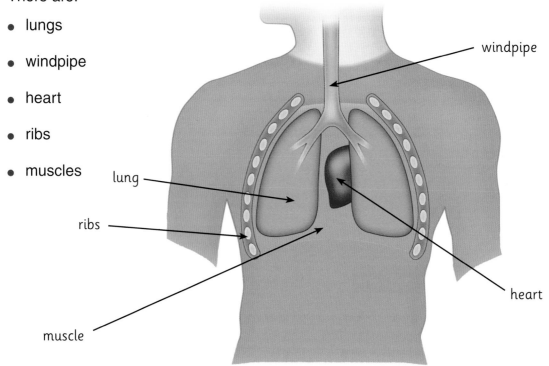

The lungs are the organs in the body that allow us to breathe. They are like balloons. They can expand and contract.

This is how it works.

1 We breathe in and our lungs fill with air and expand.

2 Blood comes from the heart and picks up the oxygen from the air in our lungs.

3 The blood delivers carbon dioxide to the lungs.

4 We breathe out and our lungs contract.

5 When we breathe out, we get rid of the carbon dioxide.

Write

Understanding the text

1 List the parts inside your chest.

2 How many lungs do you have?

3 What are the lungs surrounded by?

4 When we breathe in, what do our lungs fill with?

5 When we breathe out, what do we get rid of?

Looking at language

6 Explain these words as they are used in the text.
Use a dictionary to help you.

    a windpipe   **b** ribs   **c** expand

    d air   **e** oxygen   **f** carbon dioxide

7 The writer uses a simile to describe the lungs.
  a What is the simile he uses?
  b Do you think it is a good comparison or not?

Exploring the information

8 Why do you think the lungs are surrounded by the ribs?

9 What is the purpose of this piece of writing?

10 Why has the writer used:
  a a diagram?   **b** numbers?

11 Did you find the explanation easy to understand or not? Give your reasons.

Taking it further

▶ (RB, Unit 6, Extension)

12 Look carefully at the explanation.
What else would you like to know about the lungs and how they work?
Make a list of questions. Can you find the answers?

Write

Bigfoot

WINNER - Best Motion Picture ★ WINNER - Best Actor ★ WINNER - Best Soundtrack

'SUPERB! If you only see one film this year, see **BIGFOOT**'. (*The Daily News*)
'Gripping – it will keep you on the edge of your seat!' (*The World*)

Starring SEBASTIAN CONWAY ELLA PRINCE BRAD EVANS

BIGFOOT

In the frozen wastes of North America, a man comes face to face with a legend. He has hunted and found Bigfoot. But now, the tables are turned and the hunter becomes the hunted!
BASED ON THE BOOK BY **JOHN REEVE**

12A

BIGFOOT

A large ape-like creature has been spotted in North America. Is this just another hoax or does Bigfoot really exist? Explorer and adventurer Sam Grant is determined to find out. He will hunt Bigfoot and bring it back alive! But his adventure turns into a deadly battle with the monster! Who will win? Who will survive?

Praise for John Reeve's Bigfoot
'The best book I've read this year.'
'A real page turner.'
'I read it in one go – I couldn't put it down.'

0 123456 789010

Understanding the text

1 What is the title of the film and the book?

2 Who is the author of the book?

3 Who is starring in the film?

4 Who can go to see the film?

5 Who is the main character in the book?

Looking at language

6 Explain the meaning of these phrases in your own words.

   a keep you on the edge of your seat   **b** the tables are turned
   c a real page turner

7 Explain the meaning of these words as they are used on the film poster and the book blurb. Use a dictionary to help you.

   a soundtrack   **b** superb   **c** gripping   **d** hoax

Exploring persuasive writing

8 Why do you think the film poster includes information about awards and quotes from newspapers?

9 What sort of people do you think would go to see this film?

10 Would the poster persuade you to see the film or not? Explain your reasons.

11 Why do you think the book blurb asks questions but gives no answers?

12 Why do you think the book blurb does not tell you how the story ends?

13 Look at 'Praise for John Reeve's *Bigfoot*'. Do these comments make you want to read the book or not? Explain your reasons.

14 What are the film poster and book blurb trying to do?

Taking it further

▶ (RB, Unit 7, Extension)

15 Imagine you have seen the film *Bigfoot*. You did not think it was very good. You want to persuade your friends *not* to see it. What words and phrases would you use?

Teach

JOHN CHRISTOPHER
TRIPODS
TRILOGY

Now a major TV series

The Tripods are Coming!

The Tripods are Coming!

THE TRIPODS ARE HERE!

Massive, alien machines, the Tripods have ruled Earth for hundreds of years and enslaved the minds and bodies of most adults through the silvery caps they make them wear.

Determined to escape the ritual Capping ceremony, Will Parker runs away, heading for the distant White Mountains and the small rebel camp there, hoping to join their desperate attempts to overthrow the rule of the Tripods. The journey is long, the missions dangerous and the hope of surviving very slim . . .

John Christopher's almost unbearably exciting trilogy appears for the first time in one volume:

**The White Mountains,
The City of Gold and Lead,
The Pool of Fire**

0 123456 789010

Understanding the text

1 What is the title of the book?

2 Who is the author?

3 Where could you watch a series based on the book?

4 What are the names of the machines that rule the Earth?

5 Who is the main character in the book?

Looking at language

6 Explain the meaning of these phrases in your own words.

    a desperate attempts   **b** very slim   **c** unbearably exciting

7 Explain the meaning of these words as they are used in the book blurb. Use a dictionary to help you.

    a alien   **b** enslaved   **c** ritual
    d rebel   **e** overthrow   **f** trilogy

Exploring persuasive writing

8 Would the front cover of the book make you pick it up to see what it was about? Why? Why not?

9 Look at the yellow, orange and red writing of the book blurb. Does it make you want to read the book or not? Explain your reasons.

10 What will the 'ritual Capping ceremony' do to Will?

11 Why do you think the book blurb says that the rebels' hope of surviving is 'very slim'?

12 Why do you think the writer has used these words?

    a thrilling   **b** dangerous   **c** unbearably exciting

13 Does the book cover and blurb want to make you read the book? Why? Why not?

Taking it further

▶ (RB, Unit 7, Extension)

14 Using the information on the book cover and in the blurb, make a newspaper advert for the TV series.

Talk

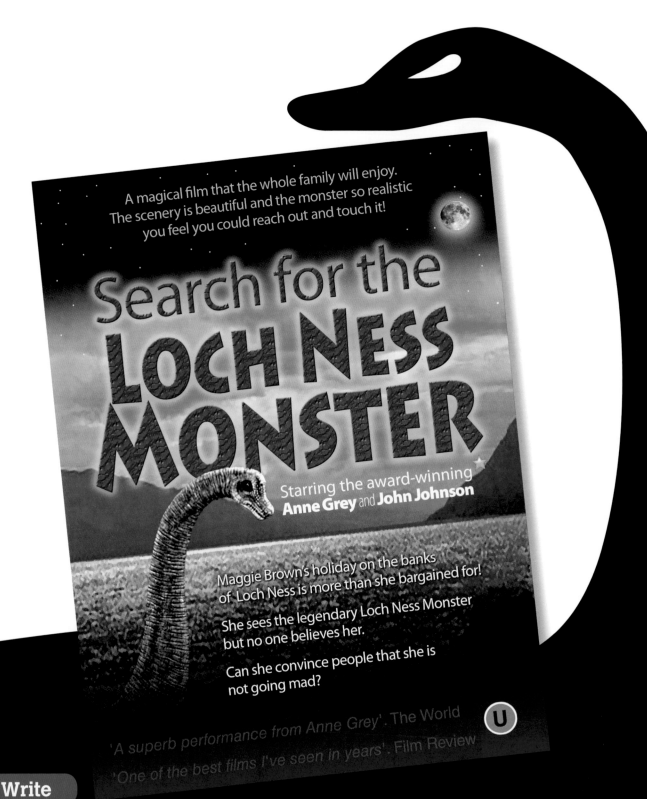

A magical film that the whole family will enjoy. The scenery is beautiful and the monster so realistic you feel you could reach out and touch it!

Search for the LOCH NESS MONSTER

Starring the award-winning **Anne Grey** and **John Johnson**

Maggie Brown's holiday on the banks of Loch Ness is more than she bargained for!

She sees the legendary Loch Ness Monster but no one believes her.

Can she convince people that she is not going mad?

'A superb performance from Anne Grey'. The World

'One of the best films I've seen in years'. Film Review

U

Write

1 What is the film being advertised?

2 Who are the stars of the film?

3 Where is the film set?

4 Who is the main character?

5 Who can go to see the film?

Looking at language

6 Explain these phrases in your own words.

    a more than she bargained for   **b** award-winning   **c** not going mad

7 Explain these words as they are used in the poster.
Use a dictionary to help you.

    a realistic   **b** legendary   **c** convince

Exploring persuasive writing

8 Find the question in the poster. Why do you think it asks that question?

9 Why do you think the poster includes quotes from newspapers?

10 Why do you think it does not include quotes from people who did not like the film?

11 Why do you think it is important that the monster is 'realistic'?

12 Would the poster persuade you to see the film? Why? Why not?

13 Do you think that Maggie convinces people that she has seen the monster? Why? Why not?

Taking it further

▶ (RB, Unit 7, Extension)

14 Imagine that *Search for the Loch Ness Monster* is a book. Write a book blurb to persuade people to read it.   **Write**

UNIT 8

Into the Forest

Frodo, Merry and Pippin are hobbits. They are on a long and dangerous journey. They come to the beginning of a huge, dark forest. There is no way around it. They have to go through it!

Looking ahead, they could see only tree-trunks of innumerable sizes and shapes: straight or bent, twisted, leaning, squat or slender, smooth or gnarled and branched. All the stems were green or grey with moss and slimy, shaggy growths.

Merry alone seemed fairly cheerful. 'You had better lead on and find a path,' Frodo said to him. 'Don't let us lose one another...'

They picked a way among the trees, and their ponies plodded along, carefully avoiding the many writhing and interlacing roots. There was no undergrowth. The ground was rising steadily, and as they went forward it seemed that the trees became taller, darker, and thicker. There was no sound, except an occasional drip of moisture falling through the still leaves. For the moment, there was no whispering or movement among the branches; but they all got an uncomfortable feeling that they were being watched with disapproval... The feeling steadily grew, until they found themselves looking up quickly, or glancing back over their shoulders, as if they expected a sudden blow.

There was not, as yet, any sign of a path, and the trees seemed constantly to bar their way...

Frodo began to wonder if it were possible to find a way through, and if he had been right to make the others come into this abominable wood.

The Lord of the Rings, **J R R Tolkien**

Teach

Understanding the text

1 What are the names of the three hobbits?
2 How were the hobbits travelling?
3 What was the only sound in the forest?
4 What was there no sign of?
5 What did Frodo begin to think?

Looking at language

6 Explain the meaning of these words as they are used in the story.
  Use a dictionary to help you.

  a innumerable   **b** squat   **c** gnarled
  d interlacing   **e** disapproval   **f** abominable

7 Find a word in the story that means the same as these.

  a keeping away from   **b** going up   **c** taking a quick look

8 Find adverbs in the story that tell you:
  a how the ponies plodded.
  b how the uncomfortable feeling grew.
  c how they looked up.
  d how the trees seemed to bar their way.

Exploring the story

9 Where is this part of the story set?
10 Why do you think 'there was no undergrowth'?
11 What do you think might have happened if the hobbits had lost one another?
12 Who do you think is the leader of the group? Explain your reasons.
13 Why do you think Frodo told Merry to go ahead and 'find a path'?
14 What do you think happens next? Do the hobbits find their way out of the wood? Do they get lost? What happens?

Taking it further   ▶ (RB, Unit 8, Extension)

15 Imagine you are with the hobbits on their journey. Write about your thoughts and feelings:
  a before you go into the forest.
  b in the forest.
  c when you come out of the forest.

Teach

Down the Rabbit Hole

Alice had been sitting by the river reading her book. Suddenly she saw something very strange – a White Rabbit ran by saying, 'Oh dear! Oh dear! I shall be too late.' Alice jumped up and followed the White Rabbit and found herself falling down a rabbit hole! Down, down, down until she landed on a heap of sticks and dry leaves.

Alice was not a bit hurt, and she jumped up on to her feet in a moment; she looked up, but it was all dark overhead. Before her was another long passage and the White Rabbit was still in sight, hurrying down it. There was not a moment to be lost. Away went Alice like the wind, and she was just in time to see the Rabbit turn a corner and say, 'Oh my ears and whiskers, how late it's getting!' Alice was close behind it when she turned the corner, but the Rabbit was no longer to be seen.

She found herself in a long, low hall which was lit up by a row of lamps hanging from the roof. There were doors all around the hall, but they were all locked. When Alice had been all the way down one side and up the other, trying every door, she walked sadly down the middle, wondering how she was ever going to get out again.

Suddenly, she came upon a little three-legged table, all made of solid glass. There was nothing on it except a tiny, golden key. Alice's first thought was that it might belong to one of the doors of the hall. But either the locks were too large or the key was too small. At any rate, it would not open any of them.

However, on the second time around, she came upon a low curtain she had not noticed before. Behind it was a little door about fifteen inches high. She tried the little golden key in the lock and, to her great delight, it fitted!

Alice opened the door and found that it led into a small passage not much larger than a rat hole. She knelt down and looked along the passage into the loveliest garden you ever saw. How she longed to get out of that dark hall and wander about among those beds of bright flowers and those cool fountains, but she couldn't even get her head through the doorway. 'And even if my head would go through,' thought poor Alice, 'it would be of very little use without my shoulders. Oh, how I wish I could shut up like a telescope! I think I could, if only I knew how to begin.' For you see, so many out-of-the-way things had happened lately, that Alice had begun to think that very few things indeed were really impossible.

Alice in Wonderland, **Lewis Carroll**

Talk

Understanding the text

1 What was the first unusual thing that happened?
2 What did Alice do?
3 Where did she find herself?
4 What was on the table?
5 Which door could Alice open?

Looking at language

6 Explain what these phrases mean as they are used in the story.

    a not a moment to be lost   **b** like the wind

    c at any rate   **d** out-of-the-way things

7 What adjectives does the writer use to describe:

    a the passage?   **b** the hall?   **c** the garden?

Exploring the story

8 What are the four settings in this extract?
9 How do you think Alice felt when:
    a she saw the White Rabbit?
    b she could not open any of the doors?
    c she found the key?
    d the key would not fit any of the doors?
10 How do you know Alice was really pleased when the key fitted the lock in the small door?
11 What did Alice see through the small door?
12 Alice wanted to get smaller so she could fit through the small door. What did she want to do?
13 What kind of person do you think Alice is? Explain your reasons.

Taking it further

▶ (RB, Unit 8, Extension)

14 Alice has fallen down the rabbit hole. She wants to get out. Think carefully about how she could:
    a get back up the hole   OR   **b** find another way out.
Remember, this is a fantasy story. Anything can happen! She can find anything that she might need and other characters can come along to help her.
Get Alice out of the rabbit hole in the most exciting and unusual way you can think of.

Talk

Lucy Looks into a Wardrobe

Lucy and her brothers and sister are playing hide and seek. Lucy decides to hide in an old wardrobe and she discovers something very unusual!

'This must be a simply enormous wardrobe!' thought Lucy, going still further in and pushing the soft folds of the coats aside to make room for her. Then she noticed that there was something crunching under her feet. 'I wonder is that more moth-balls?' she thought, stooping down to feel it with her hand. But instead of feeling the hard, smooth wood of the floor of the wardrobe, she felt something soft and powdery and extremely cold. 'This is very queer,' she said, and went on a step or two further.

Next moment she found that what she was rubbing against her face and hands was no longer soft fur but something hard and rough and even prickly. 'Why, it is just like branches of trees!' exclaimed Lucy. And then she saw that there was a light ahead of her; not a few inches away where the back of the wardrobe ought to have been, but a long way off. Something cold and soft was falling on her. A moment later she found that she was standing in the middle of a wood at night-time with snow under her feet and snowflakes falling through the air.

Lucy felt a little frightened, but she felt very inquisitive and excited as well. She looked back over her shoulder and there, between the dark tree trunks, she could still see the open doorway of the wardrobe and even catch a glimpse of the empty room from which she had set out. (She had, of course, left the door open, for she knew that it is a very silly thing to shut oneself into a wardrobe.) It seemed to be still daylight there. 'I can always get back if anything goes wrong,' thought Lucy. She began to walk forward, crunch-crunch over the snow and through the wood towards the other light. In about ten minutes she reached it and found it was a lamp-post. As she stood looking at it, wondering why there was a lamp-post in the middle of a wood and wondering what to do next, she heard a pitter patter of feet coming towards her. And soon after that a very strange person stepped out from among the trees into the light of the lamp-post.

He was only a little taller than Lucy herself and he carried over his head an umbrella, white with snow. From the waist upwards he was like a man, but his legs were shaped like a goat's (the hair on them was glossy black) and instead of feet he had goat's hoofs.

The Lion, the Witch and the Wardrobe,
C S Lewis

Understanding the text

1 Why did Lucy go into the wardrobe?

2 At first, she felt fur coats. What did she feel next?

3 Where did Lucy find herself?

4 What was the light she saw?

5 What was unusual about the 'strange person'?

Looking at language

6 Explain the meaning of these words as they are used in the story.
Use a dictionary to help you.

    a discovers   **b** stooping   **c** exclaimed
    d inquisitive   **e** glimpse   **f** glossy

7 Find the nouns in the story that are described in this way.

    a hard, smooth   **b** powdery and extremely cold
    c hard and rough and even prickly **d** dark

Exploring the story

8 What are the two settings in the extract?

9 We are told Lucy feels 'inquisitive' and 'excited'. Explain why you think she feels like this.

10 How does Lucy think she can get back 'if anything goes wrong'?

11 How do you think Lucy felt when she saw the 'strange person'?

12 What do you think:
    a Lucy said to the strange person?
    b the strange person said to Lucy?

13 What kind of person is Lucy? Explain why you think this.

Taking it further

 (RB, Unit 8, Extension)

14 Imagine you are playing hide and seek. You hide in an old wardrobe.
Lucy's wardrobe led to a wood at night where it was snowing.
Where does your wardrobe lead?
Describe what you see on the other side of your wardrobe.

Write

An Unexpected Meeting

Scene: A wood in Narnia on the other side of the wardrobe.

Lucy: Good evening.

Faun: *(bowing)* Good evening, good evening. Excuse me – I don't want to be inquisitive – but should I be right in thinking that you are a Daughter of Eve?

Lucy: *(not quite understanding)* My name's Lucy.

Faun: But you are – forgive me – you are what they call a girl?

Lucy: Of course I'm a girl.

Faun: You are in fact Human?

Lucy: *(puzzled)* Of course I'm human.

Faun: To be sure, to be sure. How stupid of me! But I've never seen a Son of Adam or a Daughter of Eve before. I am delighted. That is to say – *(hesitates)*. Delighted, delighted. Allow me to introduce myself. My name is Tumnus.

Lucy: I am very pleased to meet you, Mr Tumnus.

Faun: And may I ask, O Daughter of Eve, how you have come into Narnia?

Lucy: Narnia? What's that?

Faun: *(waving his arm around)* This is the land of Narnia, where we are now; all that lies between the lamp-post and the great castle of Cair Paravel on the eastern sea. And you – you have come from the wild woods of the west?

Lucy: I – I got in through the wardrobe in the spare room.

Faun: *(sadly)* Ah! If only I had worked harder at geography when I was a little faun, I should no doubt know all about those strange countries. It is too late now.

Lucy: *(almost laughing)* But they aren't countries at all! *(turning round)* It's only just back there – at least – I'm not sure. It is summer there.

Faun: Meanwhile, it is winter in Narnia, and has been for ever so long, and we shall both catch cold if we stand here talking in the snow. Daughter of Eve from the far land of Spare Oom, where eternal summer reigns around the bright city of War Drobe, how would it be if you came and had tea with me?

Lucy: *(Lucy shakes her head)* Thank you very much, Mr Tumnus, but I was wondering whether I ought to be getting back.

Adapted from *The Lion, the Witch and the Wardrobe*, **C S Lewis**

Understanding the text

1 Where is the scene set?
2 Who are the characters in the play?
3 Where does the land of Narnia stretch from and to?
4 What is the weather like in Narnia?
5 What does Mr Tumnus invite Lucy to do?

Looking at language

6 Explain the meaning of these words as they are used in the playscript.
  Use a dictionary to help you.

  a inquisitive　　**b** delighted　　**c** eternal　　**d** reigns

7 Explain these phrases in your own words.

  a right in thinking　　**b** to be sure　　**c** ever so long

Exploring the playscript

8 How can you tell which character is speaking?
9 Give an example of a stage direction that:
  a tells the actor what to do.
  b tells the actor how to say the words.
10 How do you know that Mr Tumnus is very polite?
11 Think of at least two reasons why Lucy thought she ought to be getting back.
12 How do you know that Mr Tumnus did not understand what 'wardrobe' and 'spare room' meant?
13 What stage directions would you write to show the actors how to say these lines?
  a Of course I'm a girl.
  b I am very pleased to meet you, Mr Tumnus.
  c Narnia? What's that?
14 What stage direction would you write to show the actor what to do while saying: '…how would it be if you came and had tea with me?'

Taking it further

▶ RB, Unit 9, Extension

15 Lucy goes back with Mr Tumnus and has tea. What do you think they talk about?
  What might Lucy want to know about him and Narnia?
  What might Mr Tumnus want to know about Lucy?

Teach

The Threat

Davy is being bullied by Webbo and his mates. Mr Clarke, the teacher, senses that something is wrong.

Scene: A classroom. The lesson has just ended and the class are leaving.

Mr Clarke:	Davy? Pop over here a sec. *Mr Clarke looks at Davy. Davy remains silent.* Any problems, Davy?
Davy:	What do you mean Mr Clarke?
Mr Clarke:	Is somebody giving you a hard time? *Davy shrugs.* You don't seem very happy. You're not taking much care with your work, either. I've noticed a change over the last couple of weeks. Would you like to tell me about it? *Davy sees Webbo peering through the classroom window. He lowers his eyes.*
Mr Clarke:	Davy?
Davy:	Yes, Mr Clarke?
Mr Clarke:	I asked if you'd like to tell me about it? I want to help. *Davy remains silent.* I can't do anything unless you tell me what's wrong, you know. *Webbo and his mates are jabbing their fingers at Davy behind Mr Clarke's back.*
Davy:	*(mumbling)* There's nothing wrong.
Mr Clarke:	*(not convinced)* Sure? *Davy nods.* OK, off you go. *Outside the classroom. Webbo and his mates are waiting.*
Webbo:	What did Clarkey want?
Davy:	He asked me if anything was wrong.
Webbo:	What did you say?
Davy:	I said no.
Vincent:	You took a long time to say no.
Davy:	He kept asking me. I didn't say anything, honest.
Webbo:	*(menacingly)* Well, keep your mouth shut or you'll really get it.

Talk

Adapted from *Chicken*, **Alan Gibbons**

Understanding the text

1 Who is Mr Clarke?
2 Why does he want to talk to Davy?
3 Who is peering through the classroom window?
4 What does Davy say is wrong?
5 What did Webbo want to know?

Looking at language

6 Explain the meaning of these words as they are used in the playscript. Use a dictionary to help you.

    a shrugs   **b** mumbling   **c** not convinced   **d** menacingly

7 Explain what these phrases mean in your own words.

    a a sec   **b** a hard time   **c** couple of weeks   **d** really get it

Exploring the playscript

8 Where is the scene set?
9 Who are the characters?
10 Pick out a stage direction that tells you:
    a how a character says something.
    b what a character does.
11 What impression do you get of Mr Clarke?
12 Why do you think Davy doesn't tell Mr Clarke what is wrong?
13 Why do you think Webbo and his mates are 'jabbing their fingers' at Davy through the classroom window?
14 Write stage directions to show how the characters say these words:
    a Any problems, Davy?
    b What did Clarkey want?
    c I didn't say anything, honest.

Taking it further

▶ RB, Unit 9, Extension

15 Imagine Davy goes back to Mr Clarke and tells him what is wrong.
Mr Clarke tells Davy what he is going to do about it.
Write, practise and perform the scene.

Talk

Staying Together

During the Second World War, many cities were bombed so children were sent away to the country for safety. Carrie and Nick and other children have been sent to Wales.

Scene: A village hall, somewhere in Wales during the Second World War.
The children have been told to stand by the wall and wait for someone to choose them.

Carrie: *(bewildered)* What's happening?

Albert: *(sounding disgusted)* A kind of cattle auction, it seems.
Albert sits on his suitcase and begins to read a book.

Woman: Nice little girl for Mrs Davies, now?
Carrie and Nick hold hands tightly. They do not want to be separated.

Carrie: *(to Nick)* Why don't you smile and look nice!
Nick blinks in surprise.
Oh, it's all right, I'm not cross. I won't leave you.
A few minutes pass and children are chosen and led away.

Woman: *(stopping in front of Carrie and Nick)* Surely you can take two, Mrs Evans?

Mrs Evans: Two girls, perhaps. Not a boy and a girl, I'm afraid. I've only one room, see, and my brother's particular.

Carrie: *(shyly)* Nick sleeps in my room at home because he has bad dreams sometimes. I always look after him and he's no trouble at all.

Mrs Evans: *(looking doubtful)* Well, I don't know what my brother will say. Perhaps I can chance it. *She smiles at Carrie.* There's pretty eyes you have, girl! Like green glass!

Carrie: *(smiling back)* Oh, Nick's the pretty one really.

Write

Adapted from *Carrie's War,*
Nina Bawden

Understanding the text

1 When is the scene set?

2 Where is it set?

3 Who are the characters?

4 Why do Carrie and Nick 'hold hands tightly'?

5 Why does Nick sleep in Carrie's room at home?

Looking at language

6 Explain the meaning of these words as they are used in the story. Use a dictionary to help you.

    a bewildered   **b** auction   **c** separated   **d** doubtful

Exploring the playscript

7 Pick out a stage direction that tells you:
   a how a character says something.
   b what a character does.

8 How do you know that Albert is not impressed with what is happening?

9 Why do you think that Carrie wants Nick to 'smile and look nice'?

10 How does Carrie try to persuade Mrs Evans to take her and her brother?

11 What impression do you get of:
   a Mrs Evans?
   b Mrs Evans's brother?

12 How do you know that Nick is usually the one people take notice of?

13 If you had been one of the children waiting to be chosen, explain how you think you would have been feeling.

Taking it further

▶ (RB, Unit 9, Extension)

14 Imagine you are Carrie. Write a letter to your mother describing what happened in the village hall and how you felt about it.

Write

UNIT 10

Burning Heat

That summer, in 1947, the rains were late. Each day seemed hotter than the last in the little village in Punjal. The earth was scorched and every weed on it had withered. The water in the canals that criss-crossed the fields was all gone, and the clay lay cracked into smooth, pink tiles. The sky was yellow, the sun hidden by dust.

The nights, too, were so hot that it was difficult to sleep at all. As long ago as April, the family had moved its beds out into the courtyard for some cool night air. In May, they carried them up to the flat roof of their white house, to catch the few faint breezes that rose some-where in the mango grove by the canal and murmured over the housetops.

In July, there were a few showers. The family had to wake up in the middle of the night, roll up their bedclothes and carry them down to the house and spread them out on the floor for the rest of the night. Zuni hated these nights, for it was stifling in the room with the small windows, and she wished she were allowed to stay out on the roof and feel the cool raindrops patter down on her hot, dry, dusty body. Her skin was covered with prickly heat that was raw and red and itched terribly.

In August, the heat grew worse. Night after night, the family tossed and turned on their beds, getting up every now and then to drink from the earthen jar in a corner of the parapet that kept the water cool when the hot summer wind was blowing, but was now, on these airless, dull nights, warm and tasteless.

On the other rooftops, too, families were spread out on their cots. They could not sleep. Some sat in the faint starlight, playing their flutes. Some talked in low murmurs, in worried voices. Others paced the rooftops – white figures in the dark, slowly walking up and down, up and down, waiting for a breeze or a cloud – so Zuni thought. She knew they were waiting, but she did not really know what they were waiting for, nor did she know why they were so worried.

One night, when Zuni had fallen asleep very late out of sheer tiredness from tossing and turning on the burning hot bed, she was woken up by a heat worse than any she had known before, and voices – low and urgent close to her, but loud and wild in the distance where the bazaar was.

'What?' she cried, sitting up, feeling the heat burn her body, and then she saw flames leaping up to the sky in the neighbour's courtyard, like a huge bonfire. That was why she was so hot that perspiration was running down from under her hair, over her face, soak-ing her clothes. She cried out in fear.

The Peacock Garden, **Anita Desai**

Understanding the text

1 In what year does the story begin?
2 What was the weather like in:
   a April?　　**b** May?　　**c** July?　　**d** August?
3 Where did the family sleep in April?
4 In July, why did the family sometimes sleep on the roof, and sometimes indoors?
5 What happened one night that frightened Zuni?

Looking at language

6 What do you understand by these phrases as they are used in the story?

   a the rains were late　　**b** tossed and turned

7 Explain the meaning of these words as they are used in the story.
   Use a dictionary to help you.

   a mango grove　　**b** parapet　　**c** bazaar

8 Find adjectives in the story that describe these.

   a the breezes　　**b** the water in the earthen jar　　**c** the nights in August

Exploring settings

9 Where do you think the story is set?
10 How did the rains being late affect:
   a the land?
   b the people?
11 What does the adjective 'stifling' tell you about the room?
12 Why do you think the people were worried?
13 Why do you think the voices were 'urgent'?
14 Would you like to live in a hot country like Zuni? Why? Why not?

Taking it further

▶ (RB, Unit 10, Extension)

15 What do you think Zuni and her family did when they saw the fire?

Teach

The Long Road

*Naledi and Tiro lived in a village 300 kilometres away from Johannesburg.
They were looked after by their granny because their father was dead and
their mother worked in Johannesburg. Their little baby sister fell ill and they set
out on foot to find their mother.*

The children walked quickly away from the village. The road was really just a
track made by car tyres. Two lines of dusty red earth leading out across the
flat dry grassland.

Once at the big tar road, they turned in the direction of the early morning
sun, for that was the way to Johannesburg. The steel railway line glinted
alongside the road.

'If only we had some money to buy tickets for the train. We don't have even
one cent.' Tiro sighed.

'Never mind. We'll get there somehow!' Naledi was still confident as they set
off eastwards. The tar road burnt their feet.

'Let's walk at the side,' Tiro suggested.

The grass was dry and scratchy, but they were used to it. Now and again,
a car or a truck roared by, and then the road was quiet again and they were
alone. Naledi began to sing the words of her favourite tune and Tiro was soon
joining in.

On they walked.

'Can't we stop and eat?' Tiro was beginning to feel sharp stabs of hunger.
But Naledi wanted to go on until they reached the top of the long, low
hill ahead.

Their legs slowed as they began the walk uphill, their bodies feeling heavy.
At last they came to the top and flopped down to rest.

Hungrily they ate their sweet potatoes and drank the water. The air was hot
and still. Some birds skimmed lightly across the sky as they gazed down at the
long road ahead. It stretched into the distance, between fenced-off fields and
dry grass, up to another far-off hill.

'Come on! We must get on,' Naledi insisted, pulling herself up quickly.

She could tell that Tiro was already tired, but they couldn't afford to stop for
long. The sun had already passed its midday position and they didn't seem to
have travelled very far.

On they walked, steadily, singing to break the silence.

Journey to Jo'burg, **Beverley Naidoo**

Talk

Understanding the text

1 Where were the children walking to?
2 Why didn't they go by train?
3 Why did they walk on the 'dry and scratchy' grass?
4 Where did they stop for something to eat?
5 What did they eat?

Looking at language

6 Explain these phrases in your own words.

   a on foot   **b** sharp stabs of hunger   **c** break the silence

7 Explain the meaning of these words as they are used in the story.
   Use a dictionary to help you.

   a grassland   **b** glinted   **c** confident
   d eastwards   **e** flopped down   **f** distance

Exploring the story

 8 Where is this part of the story set?
 9 Find evidence in the story that tells you it was very hot.
10 Which of the children do you think was older? Why?
11 Why do you think they sang as they walked?
12 Why do you think the author repeats, 'On they walked'?
13 How do you know they had been walking for more than an hour?
14 Do you think they will make it to Johannesburg? Why? Why not?

Taking it further

▶ (RB, Unit 10, Extension)

15 Imagine you are going on a journey on foot. Think about:
    a how you plan your journey.
    b what you would take with you.

    Remember! You have to carry anything you take with you.

Talk

My Home

Juan describes the beautiful scenery, animals, the people and life in the place where he was born – his home town, San Pablo.

My name is Juan. I live in Guatemala, in the mountains. My town, San Pablo, has three huge volcanoes near it, and high cliffs all around it, and steep, bright green fields of corn and garlic and onions growing in the hills, and red coffee berries growing in the shade of big trees in the valleys. It has lots of flowers and birds – eagles and orioles and owls, hummingbirds, and flocks of wild parrots that zoom down out of the trees to steal our corn and don't talk any language but their own.

San Pablo is on a big lake with seven other towns around it. People get from one town to another mostly by ferry-boat or canoe. There's a road, but it's not a good one.

I've never been in any of the other towns, only San Pablo. Still, at night I like to go down to the lake and look at the lights of the fishing canoes on the black water, and the lights of the other towns glowing at us across the lake, and the thousands of stars in the sky. It seems like every light is saying, 'You're not alone. We're here too.'

Right in town, San Pablo has stray dogs and dust in the street, and a few cars,

and a few buses from the big cities, and a few mules carrying firewood from the mountains, and lots of people carrying still more stuff – jugs of water or big baskets of bread or vegetables on their heads, babies on their backs, or sometimes huge wooden beams balanced over their shoulders – whatever they need to take home. Since there aren't many cars, if you want something, you carry it yourself, no matter how heavy it is.

The only time people aren't carrying things is at night, when they go out just to stroll around town and have fun and tell stories and talk to their friends. Everybody walks in the street, more or less straight down the middle, and if a car comes while somebody's having a good conversation or telling a good story, the car has to wait till the story finishes before the people will move out of the way. Stories are important here, and cars aren't.

Down by the beach there's an especially beautiful place – a big, low house with lots of windows, and flowers and palm trees all around, and green grass and peacocks in the yard, and an iron gate that opens for walking right down to the water.

That's where I was born.

The Most Beautiful Place in the World,
Ann Cameron

1 Give two examples from the story of:
   a things that grow in the hills.
   b birds.
   c things that people carry.

2 How do people get from town to town?

3 Why don't they use the road?

4 What do people do at night in San Pablo?

5 Why does Juan say that the house on the beach is an 'especially beautiful place'?

Looking at language

6 Explain these phrases from the story in your own words.

   a stray dogs   b strolled around   c more or less

7 Explain the meaning of these words as they are used in the story. Use a dictionary to help you.

   a zoom   b mules   c beams   d conversation

8 Find adjectives in the story that describe these.

   a the fields   b the lake   c the beams

Exploring the setting

9 Could San Pablo be a dangerous place to live? Why?

10 How can you tell San Pablo has a hot climate?

11 Do you think San Pablo is a rich town or a poor town? Explain your reasons.

12 What can Juan see at night:
   a in the sky?   b across the water?

13 Do you think Juan would like to visit other places or not? Explain your reasons.

14 How do you think the writer wants the reader to feel about where he was born?

Taking it further

▶ (RB, Unit 10, Extension)   Write

15 Explain what you like about San Pablo and what you don't like about it.

How to Use This Book

This heading tells you the name of the text.

The red questions are about understanding what's happened in the text.

This heading tells you about the unit topic.

The purple questions are about words and phrases used in the text.

UNIT 1

Characters' Points of View

Leaving London

Carrie, 12, and her younger brother Nick, 9, are being evacuated from London during the Second World War. They are on a train with their schoolteacher, Miss Fazackerly, going to Wales.

He threw up all over Miss Fazackerly's skirt. He had been feeling sick ever since they left the main junction and climbed into the joggling, jolting little train for the last lap of their journey, but the sudden whistle had finished him.

Such a noise – it seemed to split the sky open. 'Enough to frighten the dead,' Miss Fazackerly said, mopping her skirt and Nick's face with her handkerchief. He lay back limp as a rag and let her do it, the way he always let people do things for him, not lifting a finger. 'Poor lamb,' Miss Fazackerly said, but Carrie looked stern.

'It's all his own fault. He's been stuffing his face ever since we left London.' … He had had all her chocolate, too! 'I knew he'd be sick,' she said smugly.

'Might have warned me then, mightn't you?' Miss Fazackerly said. Not unkindly, she was one of the kindest teachers in the school, but Carrie wanted to cry suddenly. If she had been Nick she would have cried, or at least put on a hurt face. Being Carrie she stared crossly out of the carriage window at the big mountain on the far side of the valley. It was brown and purple on the top and green lower down; streaked with silver trickles of water and dotted with sheep. Sheep and mountains.

'Oh, it'll be such fun,' their mother had said when she kissed them good-bye at the station. 'Living in the country instead of the stuffy old city. You'll love it, you see if you don't!' As if Hitler had arranged this old war for their benefit, just so that Carrie and Nick could be sent away in a train with gas masks slung over their shoulders and their names on cards round their necks. Labelled like parcels – Caroline Wendy Willow and Nicholas Peter Willow – only with no address to be sent to. None of them, not even the teachers, knew where they were going. 'That's part of the adventure,' Carrie's mother had said, and not just to cheer them up: it was her nature to look on the bright side. …

Thinking of her mother, always making the best of things (or pretending to: when the train began to move she had stopped smiling), Carrie nearly did cry. There was a lump like a pill stuck in her throat. She swallowed hard and pulled faces.

The train was slowing. 'Here we are,' Miss Fazackerly said. 'Collect your things, don't leave anything. Take care of Nick, Carrie.'

Carrie's War, **Nina Bawden**

Teach

4

Understanding the text

1 Who are the main characters in the story?

2 What is the setting?

3 Where are they moving to?

4 Why has Nick been sick?

5 Where are they moving from?

Looking at language

6 Choose the correct definition for each of these phrases.

a	*finished him*	made him feel better	made him feel worse
b	*not lifting a finger*	helping	not helping
c	*look on the bright side*	be pessimistic	be optimistic

7 Explain what these words mean as they are used in the story. Use a dictionary to help you.

    a stern   **b** smugly   **c** stuffy   **d** benefit   **e** slung

Exploring the characters

8 We are told Miss Fazackerly is 'kind'. What kind things did she do?

9 What impression do you get of:

    a Carrie?   **b** Nick?

10 How do you know that the children's mother is only pretending to make the best of things?

11 Why do you think the children are being sent away from home?

Taking it further

▶ (RB, Unit I, Extension)

12 If you were Nick or Carrie would you think this was an adventure or would you be homesick? Give your reasons.

Teach

5

The author's name is here.

The green questions are about the unit topic, and may ask you to read between the lines—to work out things that the author implies but does not state.

The blue questions ask you to think more deeply about the text.

This tells you that there's an Extension resource sheet relating to this question in the Resources & Assessment Book.